D0688960

THE TWELVE DAYS OF CHRISTMAS

A CELEBRATION AND HISTORY

ILLUSTRATIONS AND TEXT BY

LEIGH GRANT

HARRY N. ABRAMS, INC., PUBLISHERS

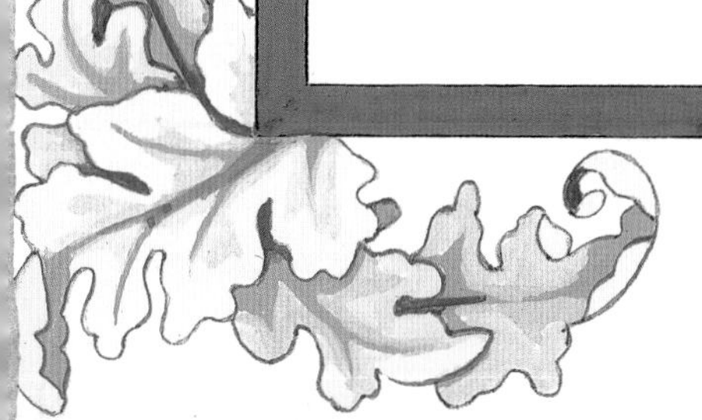

DEDICATION

For Tony, Nicholas, and Kyra whose love and encouragement made this book possible. As always, thank you.

For the rest of my family, and especially my father—stalwart supporters all. Stand fast.

Merry Christmas

EDITOR: ROBERT MORTON

TYPOGRAPHIC DESIGNER: CAROL A. ROBSON

Library of Congress Catalog Card Number: 95–75656
ISBN 0–8109–3881–2

Copyright © 1995 Leigh Grant

Published in 1995 by Harry N. Abrams, Incorporated, New York
A Times Mirror Company
All rights reserved. No part of the contents of this book may be reproduced
without the written permission of the publisher

Printed and bound in Hong Kong

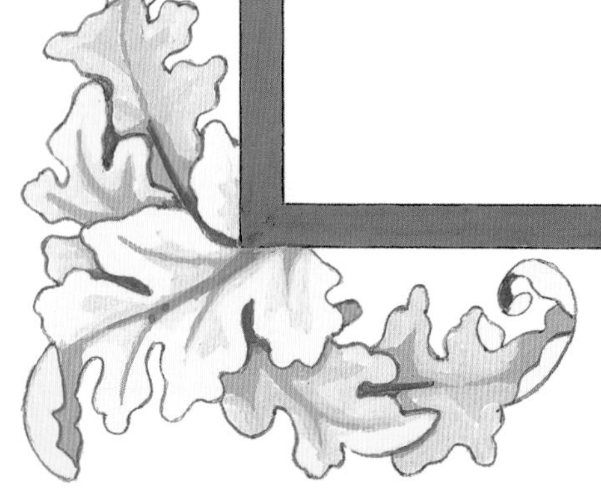

The Twelve Days of Christmas

A History

Long before the Christian era, winter was already a time of feasts and festivals. Included in these celebrations, especially those of the Roman, were the customs of bringing into the house evergreen boughs to recall the greening of spring, the giving of gifts (clay dolls, candles, or small, sweet cakes), the election of a mock king, the wearing of disguises and reversal of roles, and the welcoming of the new year with its new sun.

Although today Christmas is universally celebrated on December 25th, the true date of the Nativity remains a mystery. To the early Catholic church the important date was January 6th, Epiphany, the date of the baptism of Christ, virtually the "birth" of His soul. By the fourth century, setting a date for the Nativity had become an issue for the rapidly expanding Christian faith. Perhaps the early Christians sensed that the mysticism of faith needed a human connection, the common appeal of a child of lowly birth. Perhaps they wished to compete with the popular religion of the Mithraism, whose feast of the Invincible Sun took place on December 25th, the winter solstice on the Julian calendar.

In any case, by the early sixth century the Christian emperor Justinian had proclaimed Christmas a public holiday. The eight days of feasting allowed by the church later became twelve. By the ninth century, in England, King Alfred listed the holidays as beginning with "twelve days at Christmas," December 25th through January 6th. Originally reckoned in nights, the Twelfth Day falls on January 6, but the Twelfth Night precedes it.

Initiated by Saint Francis, the practice of staging crèches to reenact the Nativity became popular in the thirteenth century. Kings and other noblemen were attracted to the festivities by the positive image of the ancient kings, the Magi, connecting Epiphany and Christmas.

As kings prospered, so did the celebration of Christmas, which reached its apex in the late Middle Ages. In seventeenth century England, however, the Puritan Commonwealth (under Oliver Cromwell) not only toppled a king, it abolished Christmas altogether. The holiday was brought back in a more modest form by the Restoration, but it was not until the late eighteenth century in England that the revival of interest in the Middle Ages renewed the enthusiasm for the Twelve Days. By the middle of the nineteenth century, the expansion of working days brought about by the Industrial Revolution led to the final decline of the twelve day holiday, and now only the song serves as a reminder of the old ways.

The published verse for the *Twelve Days of Christmas* first appears in England in 1780 in *Mirth Without Mischief*. This tiny children's book describes a memory-and-forfeits game that was played at the time. In it, the leader recites the first verse, followed in turn by each of the players, and then adds the second verse, and so on. The forfeit demanded of a player for a missed verse or other mistake might be a kiss, a sweet, or an item of food. The game became a popular entertainment at Twelfth Night parties.

There are three versions of the song in France and another in Scotland. Although the English version was much older than its first publication, the French rhymes appear to be even earlier.

On the following pages, surrounding the illustrations, are rhymes that I have devised which suggest the essence of the eighteenth-century celebration. Beginning on page 27 are fuller explanations about the gifts, the customs, history, and folklore contained in *The Twelve Days of Christmas*.

n the first day of Christmas…

At winter solstice trees are blessed

With cider poured all' round.

For fruit abundant on the bough

Good harvest for the town.

My true love gave to me
A partridge in a pear tree.

Turtledoves

Cooed for the Babe

For whom

This holiday is made.

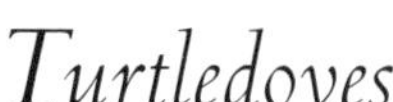

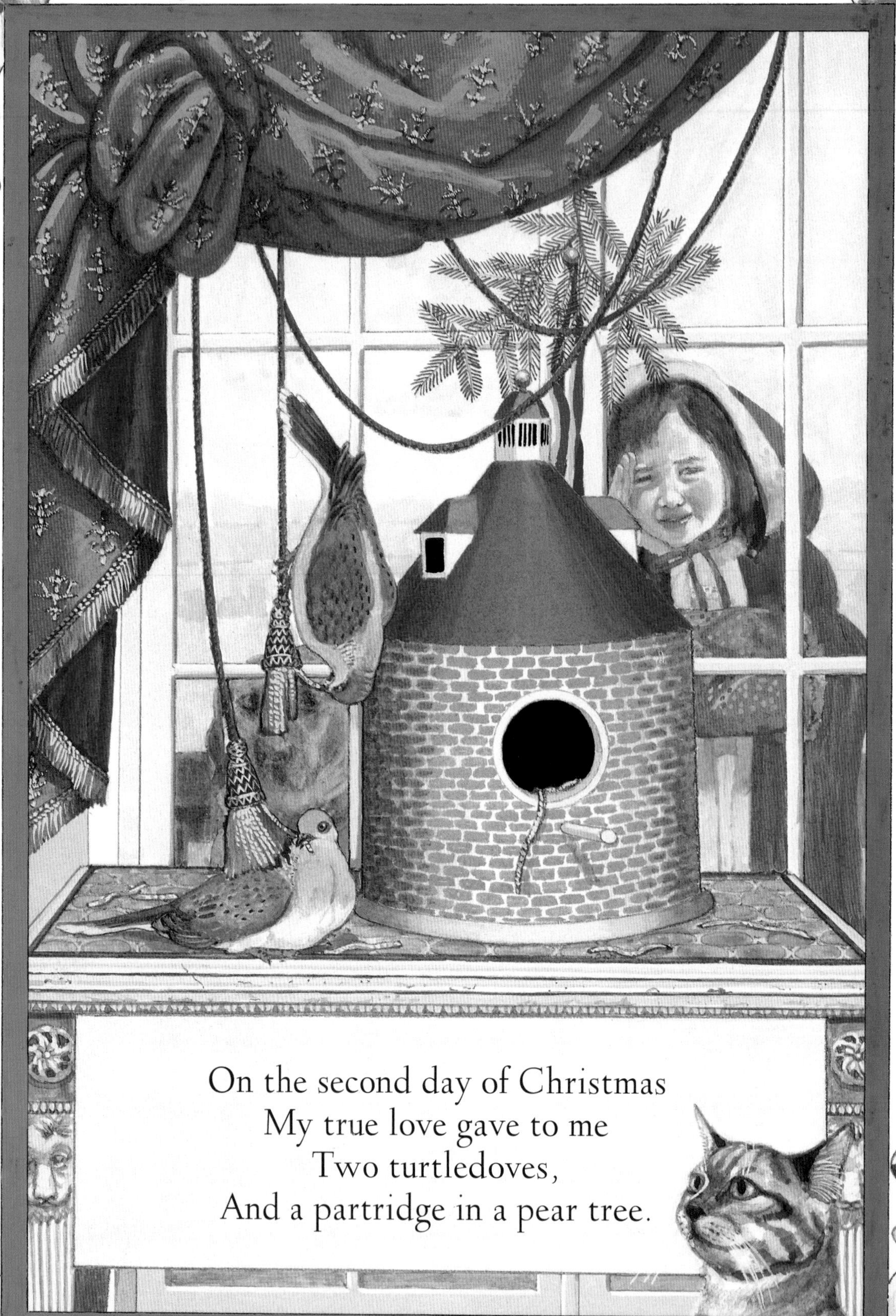

On the second day of Christmas
My true love gave to me
Two turtledoves,
And a partridge in a pear tree.

Some say this song came from a game,
Some say it springs from France.
The Breton hens uphold the last
And strut a country dance.

On the third day of Christmas
My true love gave to me
Three French hens,
Two turtledoves,
And a partridge in a pear tree.

Colly birds are black as night
But sing so sweetly in the light
And if one should happen by,
T'would be lovely in a pie.

On the fourth day of Christmas
My true love gave to me
Four calling birds,
Three French hens,
Two turtledoves,
And a partridge in a pear tree.

In this song the five gold rings
Were neck bands on a pheasant,
But for this book the artist thought,
Real gold would be more pleasant.

On the fifth day of Christmas
My true love gave to me
Five gold rings,
Four calling birds,
Three French hens,
Two turtledoves,
And a partridge in a pear tree.

The barnyard geese

For Christmas meat it's goose I'm fed.

On the sixth day of Christmas
My true love gave to me
Six geese a-laying,
Five gold rings,

upon my bed,

are loud and stout,

Four calling birds,
Three French hens,
Two turtledoves,
And a partridge in a pear tree.

Like dogs they keep intruders out.

Their down is warm

Beneath the stony gods,

The swans.

majestic things,

Graceful, white,

they glide,

Treasured captives, kept by kings.

T'is said it was

they face the East

And kneel in manner mild.

the cow's sweet breath

On the eighth day of Christmas
My true love gave to me
Eight maids a-milking,
Seven swans a-swimming,
Six geese a-laying,
Five gold rings,
Four calling birds,
Three French hens,
Two turtledoves,
And a partridge in a pear tree.

First warmed the Holy Child.

So Christmas Eve,

The waits are out

On the ninth day of Christmas
My true love gave to me
Nine drummers drumming,
Eight maids a-milking,
Seven swans a-swimming,

the player's sound

With clapping hands and marching feet.

about the town

Six geese a-laying,
Five gold rings,
Four calling birds,
Three French hens,
Two turtledoves,
And a partridge in a pear tree.

To drum their festive beat.

We welcome in

The skirl of the bagpipes

On the tenth day of Christmas
My true love gave to me
Ten pipers piping,
Nine drummers drumming,
Eight maids a-milking,
Seven swans a-swimming,
Six geese a-laying,
Five gold rings,
Four calling birds,
Three French hens,
Two turtledoves,
And a partridge in a pear tree.

remind us this day

Of the flocks safe with shepherds in fields far away.

The Scots march to war while the French dance and play,

But the drones and the chanters

could stir feet of clay.

Stamp the earth!

To banish winter's ire.

On the eleventh day of Christmas
My true love gave to me
Eleven ladies dancing,
Ten pipers piping,
Nine drummers drumming,
Eight maids a-milking,
Seven swans a-swimming,
Six geese a-laying,
Five gold rings,
Four calling birds,
Three French hens,
Two turtledoves,

we turn

Awake! Awake!

Dance round the solstice fire.

Clockwise like the sun

And a partridge in a pear tree.

Hey! Ho!

wassailing the crowd,

The company's merry, the revelry loud.

For the Lord of Misrule!

On the twelfth day of Christmas
My true love gave to me
Twelve lords a-leaping,

Play us a tune or give us a fool.

Feasting and dancing

This prince of plum cakes

good fortune's bean

For by this card, one's role is seen.

for Twelfth Night,

Eleven ladies dancing,
Ten pipers piping,
Nine drummers drumming,
Eight maids a-milking,
Seven swans a-swimming,
Six geese a-laying,
Five gold rings,
Four calling birds,
Three French hens,
Two turtledoves,

Delicious artifice of white,

No longer hides

And a partridge in a pear tree.

A PARTRIDGE IN A PEAR TREE

For fruit abundant on the bough,
Good harvest for the town.
At winter solstice trees are blessed
With cider poured all 'round.

After winter solstice the days begin to grow longer, hinting of spring. Ancient peoples were deeply affected by these changes in the natural signs. In their minds, the rebirth of the sun offered assurance of renewed fertility on earth. As the hours of daylight grew, an age-old fear of the dark subsided and the people found cause to celebrate. Twelfth Night, having been built on the framework of earlier beliefs and superstitions, still exhibits some of the old customs, when people celebrated with feasting, ritual, and sacrifice.

One ritual of Twelfth Night was wassailing the fruit trees, a fertility rite that probably dates back to the Druids. By the eighteenth century, this was done by pouring cider, honey, spices, and lamb's wool (the pulp of burst, baked apples) from a wooden wassail bowl around the trees. Wassail or "waes hael" means "be whole," roughly translated as "good health." Celebrants shared the libation and enlivened the festivities by firing shots into the branches. The noise was meant to frighten away evil spirits believed to be abroad at that time of year.

In another folk belief associated with fruit trees, a young woman's future was predicted. Walking backward three times around a pear tree on Christmas morning, a girl could gaze into the branches and perceive the image of her future husband.

Aspects of fertility and sexuality have been embodied by fruit since ancient times. The apple, for example, represents the female; the pear, the male. These associations were extended to animals as well. The male partridge, renowned as a lusty suitor who fathered numerous progeny, imparts to the verse a symbolic suggestion on the part of the giver.

In Britain the partridge best known for perching in trees was the red-legged partridge, *Alectoris rufa*, and here may lie a clue to the source of the song. This game bird was only introduced into England from France in the late 1770s, and the verse predates this, supporting those who believe in a French origin for the song.

Two turtledoves

Turtledoves
Cooed for the babe
For whom
Festivity is made.

In biblical times, the turtledove returned to Palestine annually in large flocks to breed and was considered a harbinger of spring and a symbol of seasonal rebirth.

In the arid regions of the Near East the dove has more ancient associations with both love and water, which are, in their respective ways, sources of life and therefore fertility. Astarte, the Phoenician goddess of love, was hatched on the banks of the Euphrates from an egg that was warmed by two doves. Doves drew the chariot of the Roman goddess Venus, patroness of love and beauty—also born of water. Doves are often depicted drinking at fountains.

Dovecotes were built on tombs in Babylon, and the Egyptians associated birds with the human soul. The Romans kept funerary urns near dovecotes; thus, from columba, or dove, came the word columbarium, a vault of niches containing ashes of the dead. Considering these traditions, it is not surprising that Christianity embraced the dove as the symbol of the Holy Ghost: earthly love become divine. The dove's association with water is also present in the appearance of the dove above Christ's head during baptism (Matthew), and the pagan doves on fountains reappear as symbolic Christian motifs on baptismal fonts in medieval churches. Doves are traditionally believed to have been in the stable at Bethlehem, a town honeycombed with limestone caves, favorite nesting sites for these birds. Some believe that the stable of Christ's birth was, in fact, a cave.

Dovecotes were only built in numbers in Britain after 1066, when the Norman invaders brought regulations dating back to Charlemagne that required the raising of various fowl, including turtledoves, for winter food for the nobility. Commoners, by law, were restricted to other game.

In secular terms, the billing, or "kissing," of doves has been taken as a sign that they have chosen a mate, usually for life. By the eighteenth century, turtledoves symbolized faithfulness and conjugal devotion.

THREE FRENCH HENS

Some say this song comes from a game,
Some swear it springs from France.
The Breton hens uphold the last
And strut a country dance.

The three French hens may be a play on the Latin name for France, once called Gaul, which in Latin is *Gallia*, similar to the Roman word for rooster.

Originally descended from the jungle fowl of India and Southeast Asia, the domestic chicken has a long association with worship of the sun. The cock's crowing at dawn made him the guardian of light. The Romans kept sacred chickens in their temples to use in predicting the future. Some forecasts were based on the shape and color of the fowls' livers. Other prophecies were determined by an offering of grain: hearty pecking at the grain foretold success, and the reverse signaled failure. Needless to say, it was not too difficult to control the outcome of this test. Roman generals always kept a small flock of chickens for this purpose. The Romans helped spread these birds throughout Europe and Britain, where they remained unchanged for centuries.

It is written that when Christ was born, the cock crowed "Christus natus est" in recognition of the "Light of the World." Christian tradition continues to connect the rooster with light. A rooster on a Christian tomb symbolizes resurrection.

During the eighteenth century, English and European merchants began to bring back large exotic fowl from the Orient. These were crossed with the descendants of the Roman chickens and new breeds were developed. The three hens illustrated, perhaps purchased in France, are related to the Oriental Silkie and represent new breeding stock. White chickens were said to bring good luck, and the hen was a symbol of devoted motherhood.

Four colly birds

Colly birds are black as night
But sing so sweetly in the light.
And if one should happen by,
T'would be lovely in a pie.

Colly means black as coal and is frequently replaced in the song by "calling," which is incorrect. Colly birds are European blackbirds, a type of thrush. Common throughout England, their lovely flutelike song can be heard as early as December and lasts until July.

These birds, like the others in the song, formed part of the magnificent feasts of the twelve-day celebration. The blackbird has long been a gourmet's delight. In medieval times, game was rarely eaten when it was fresh. Most birds were hung until they reached a state of decay that was considered desirable. They were then inundated with spices, and sometimes with sugar and verjuice (the acid juice of unripe plums). These marinated meats were made into that medieval favorite, the pie. Everything went into meat pies, even badgers and dormice. There is a saying in Cornwall that the devil dare not appear at Christmas for fear he might be baked into a pie.

Blackbird pies are celebrated in "Sing a Song of Sixpence" from *Mother Goose*. The proliferation of pies and exuberant displays for Twelfth Night rose to a climax just before the austere regime of Oliver Cromwell. Baroque table settings and their related entertainments featured pasteboard castles that shot tiny fireworks; ladies threw eggshells of sweet water at one another; a "surprise" pie opened to reveal live frogs and another discharged birds who flew toward the candles, plunging all into darkness and mayhem. "Sing a Song of Sixpence" may be based on the last pie.

Finally, the pie of pies was conceived for Sir Henry Grey at a Twelfth Night celebration in London in 1770. It was nine feet in circumference and contained two bushels of flour, two woodcocks, two turkeys, two rabbits, two neat's tongues (a type of ox), four geese, four ducks, four partridges, six pigeons, seven blackbirds, and twenty pounds of butter. It had to be wheeled into the dining room as it weighed 168 pounds.

Five gold rings

In this song the five gold rings
Were neck bands on a pheasant,
But for this book the artist thought
Real gold would be more pleasant.

Five gold rings refer not to jewelry, but to ring-necked pheasants. This popular game bird was also known as the English or Mongolian pheasant and is a relative of the jungle fowl, ancestor of the chicken.

The ring-necked pheasant originally ranged over Asia Minor and as far east as China and Korea, and included a subspecies that lacked the white ring around its neck. The pheasant's Latin name, *Phasianus colchicus,* has an interesting history. *Colchicus* means "of Colchis," an ancient country on the eastern edge of the Black Sea in what is now called the Caucasus. An Ionian colony called Phasis was founded there near a river of the same name. In 750 B. C., when Jason and the Argonauts sailed from Thessaly (Greece) on their epic voyage to search out the "Golden Fleece" in order to regain Jason's birthright, they landed in Phasis. They returned with the sorceress Medea and some beautiful golden birds. The English word pheasant derives from the Greek, *Phasianornis,* meaning "bird of Phasis." It is entirely possible that this subspecies of ring-necked pheasant was in fact the legendary Golden Fleece.

The Romans inherited the pheasant from the Greeks. Well known for their culinary skills, the Romans revered the fowl as a delicacy fit for their sumptuous feasts, and Emperor Elagabalus, famed for his caprice and extravagance, fed them to his lions. The Roman conquest distributed pheasants throughout Europe and Britain, where they remained objects of royal privilege.

In the Middle Ages, the serving of pheasant, like swan and peacock, was often the high point of a feast, and it became customary to swear an oath upon it. Like politicians' vows, these oaths were not always fulfilled.

The English pheasant is a mixture of the Argonauts' subspecies, with its dark neck, and the true Chinese species, *Phasianus colchicus torquatus,* which has a ringed neck. Consequently, some pheasants have a wide band (like the one in the painting), some a narrow one, and some no band at all.

Six geese a-laying

The barnyard geese are loud and stout,
Like dogs they keep intruders out.
Their down is warm upon my bed,
For Christmas meat it's goose I'm fed.

Although the goose is one of the earliest domesticated animals, dating back to Neolithic times, it was long a subject of folklore and fantasy. Before the sixteenth century, the miraculous seasonal disappearance and reappearance of geese and other migratory birds caused them to become symbols of the solar year, solstice, fertility, and rebirth. The wild goose was seen as an intermediary between this world and the next since it vanished like the sun when the days grew shorter, only to reappear as they lengthened.

The ancient Egyptians believed that when a mummified body lay in the tomb, its soul, or Ka, rose up in the form of a goose with a human head. Food was placed in the tomb for the Ka's nourishment since it was thought of as a physical being. This manifestation of the spirit followed the setting sun on a journey through the underworld and returned to the body at dawn. The journey was part of a quest for immortality.

The goose was also sacred to many deities, among them Juno, the Roman Queen of Heaven and goddess of women and marriage. In her temple, a flock of sacred geese represented domesticity and fertility. Juno's geese achieved immortality when, in 387 B.C., their noisy cackling warned Rome that the barbarians were at the gates. The intruders were repulsed and the geese became celebrated for their service.

Caesar reported that the ancient Britons kept geese for pleasure but did not eat them. Later, however, it was said that Elizabeth I was dining on goose when news was brought to her that the Spanish Armada had been defeated.

Medieval seafarers, whose vessels had limited range and never ventured very far north, noticed a similarity between a particular migratory goose and a long-necked barnacle that grew on the hulls of their ships. This goose, a winter migrant from its Arctic breeding grounds, was known only as a mature bird. The barnacle became the accepted origin of this goose, and the tale was further embellished with the information that it grew on a seaside tree. If the goslings had been seen, the association might never have been made.

The barnacle goose became a subject of theological debate when it was served at the table on holiday fast days. The argument was that since the goose came from a tree, and was, therefore, fruit, it was not forbidden as was the flesh of other fowl or beasts. By the 1500s, exploration and systematic scientific observation brought an end to the mystery and the argument.

By the eighteenth century the goose was the established centerpiece of the Christmas dinner. The boar of the medieval banquet was gone, hunted to extinction in Britain. The goose was a big bird that matured at Christmas-time —often so big that it had to be sent to the baker to be cooked in his oven. A string of sausages around the goose reminded diners of the boar's garland of old. The other big bird, the Ind-cock or turkey, was not introduced until the 1500s, and although it rivaled the goose in size, it lacked the tradition.

Seven swans a-swimming

Beneath the stony gods, they glide,
Treasured captives, kept by kings.
Graceful, white, majestic things,
The swans.

Ancient man was fascinated with waterfowl, whose mastery of both water and air bespoke a knowledge of the unknown. The dips and dives of swans, geese, and ducks on lakes, rivers, and seas hinted at familiarity with watery depths, often the site of the Underworld in early mythologies. And the mysterious migratory flights of the birds linked them with the heavens and the gods of the sky. These earthly creatures, who could pass from land into the water or the air, seemed to connect the natural and the supernatural worlds.

In Egypt, swans, like geese, were associated with the quest for immortality. In Greece, priests of the sacred rites of Demeter, the goddess of agriculture, were called swans after a ritual immersion. According to myth, the goddess Demeter had a lovely daughter, Persephone, who was abducted by the god of the underworld. In vain Demeter searched for her, neglecting her duties in her sorrow, and the earth shriveled. Finally, she paused in her search at Eleusis, where Zeus, to save the world, struck a bargain with her for the return of her daughter: for three-quarters of the year Persephone returned to the earth and Demeter would husband the land; for the other quarter, when Persephone remained below, Demeter would grieve, and nothing would grow. The rites she initiated at Eleusis were called the Eleusinian mysteries, and the priests, chosen from one family, were said to be descended from swans.

The swan myths of the Celtic tribes of Britain and Ireland echo Demeter's search. In these stories, lost loved ones have been transformed by magic into swans, the symbol of their enchantment being a gold or silver chain about their necks. The moment of transformation often coincides with the November festival of Samhain, when the gates to the otherworld opened and souls could pass freely in and out. The Celts believed that at death the soul exchanged one body for another, either human or animal. The swan myths seem to be about the journeys of these souls.

The mute swan has long been revered in England, and was the subject of many myths. Later sagas became infused with overtures of chivalry and Christian virtues by the scholar monks of Ireland. And as the legends of King Arthur were spawned in medieval times, these heroes, such as Helyas, the Swan Knight, moved into history and were claimed as forebears of kings. In Britain, King Stephen's wife, Matilda, first brought the swan as a heraldic emblem from just such an ancestry in France.

In 1304, England's King Edward I took his vow of knighthood over two white swans adorned with crowns and golden nets, emphasizing the sanctity of the occasion with the symbolic purity of the birds. By association, the swan became synonymous with royalty, and the keeping of swans was the monarch's exclusive prerogative. To this day in Britain the majestic bird remains a potent symbol of royalty at Christmas, the birthday of the "King of kings."

One swan illustrated in the painting is the black swan, discovered in Australia by the Dutch in 1697. It was subsequently introduced into Europe, where it provoked great astonishment: all European swans are white. The "stony gods" in the verse refers to the sculpture gallery that is shown, an architectural feature often found in great English houses. Objects collected for these galleries often arrived through the popular practice of sending young noblemen abroad for the Grand Tour, especially in the eighteenth century. The intent of that structured European itinerary was an education in the finer points of civilization, and an appreciation of the arts, ancient and modern. Many times the traveler became a collector.

EIGHT MAIDS A-MILKING

'Tis said it was the cow's sweet breath
First warmed the Holy Child.
So Christmas Eve, they face the East
And kneel in manner mild.

The Bible does not mention the presence of the ox and the ass in the stable at Bethlehem. They are, however, described in the Apocrypha, related texts of the period. In 1223, Francis of Assisi staged the first living crèche, manifesting his feelings for the importance of all God's creatures. This event helped foster a rich Christmas folklore throughout Europe. English tradition included the belief that cattle turned toward the East and bowed in remembrance of the Christ Child's birth. In many countries, animals were said to speak on Christmas Eve and were often fed special meals in hopes of renewed fertility for the coming year.

In the English song, the eighth gift refers to the many products of milk. Fresh milk was not often drunk in an unaltered state as it had a tendency to separate and become sour easily, but sweet milk, soured milk, cream, and cheese were indispensable ingredients in medieval recipes. (In the twelfth verse of *Les Dons de l'An*, one of the French versions of the game, twelve cheeses are the gift.)

Many milk-based foods date from the Middle Ages. One favorite was custard. Another was a mixture of hulled, boiled wheat cooked slowly in milk and colored with saffron and egg yolks. Called furmenty, it may be descended from the ritual cereal fed to victims of sacrifice in Celtic and northern European cultures.

A number of foods were made with soured milk. Adding verjuice, ale, or wine to warm milk curdled it. The curds were then spooned into a linen bag, the whey dripped into a bowl, and the resulting cottage cheese was served with salt or sugar and ginger. Posset was a sugared and spiced drink of curdled milk, hot wine, or ale to aid digestion after the banquet. There was even a curdled milk beer of Celtic ancestry whose recipe was still in use throughout the eighteenth century.

Cheeses were much prized in Britain and France and provided food for the winter months when fodder was scarce and the milk yield low. In England during the eighteenth century a curious game called "Yawning for the Chesire Cheese" was played on Christmas night. Each contestant yawned, and the one who made the widest and longest yawn—which produced the most sympathetic yawns in return—was the winner and took home the cheese, effectively ending the festivities.

Finally, asking a maid to "come a-milking" was, by the eighteenth century, tantamount to a proposal of marriage, although it sprang from an older suggestion with less honorable intention.

NINE DRUMMERS DRUMMING

The waits are out about the town
To drum their festive beat.
We welcome in the players' sound
With clapping hands and marching feet.

The waits were originally the town watchmen who called the hours of the night and patrolled the streets. By the eighteenth century, this name was commonly applied to the town musicians who walked the parish playing and were suitably rewarded, especially during Christmas festivities. Another custom of the waits at Christmas was to serenade a sleeper at midnight or even dawn.

The resounding beat of the drum is such a captivating, suggestive, and pervasive sound that it seems difficult to believe that western Europe had no true drums until the Crusaders brought them home as spoils of war from their bloody battles in the Holy Land. Although the Sumerians had danced for their mother goddess to the beat of the frame drum and the Egyptians had played a form of kettledrum, Europe inherited only the tambourine.

By the thirteenth century, the drums that the Crusaders introduced, small, paired kettledrums and the tabor, were well established. The kettledrums were similar to two pots joined in the middle and with skin covers. The British called them nakers, the French *nacaires*, from the Arabic *naqqara*. Large kettledrums became associated with nobility and war. The resonance of such drums carried into battle conveyed military codes and signals and set the pace of a march.

The tabor was a rope-tensioned drum with an upper head of calfskin (the playing surface) and a lower one with strings of gut, called snares, stretched across. It was known in later times as both a side drum, because of the way it was carried and played, and as a snare drum. (In the painting the waits are shown playing side drums.)

The medieval feast, with its orchestrated pageantry and leisurely pace, welcomed the tabor. While trumpet flourishes announced the arrival of each course, the tabor, joined with a pipe or bagpipe, furnished music for entertainment. These gay and lively tunes were suitable for dance and as accompaniment for the acrobats and jugglers who performed amidst the buzz of conversation and noisy consumption of food. Occasionally, one musician played both the pipe and the tabor, a combination known in England as "whittle and dub."

The Arab influence was seen anew in the eighteenth century, when Europe was swept with a fad for janissary bands with their highly percussive sound and exotic clothing. Janissaries were the elite fighting corps of the Turkish Empire. Their colorful costumes became the inspiration for the uniforms of marching bands.

Ten pipers piping

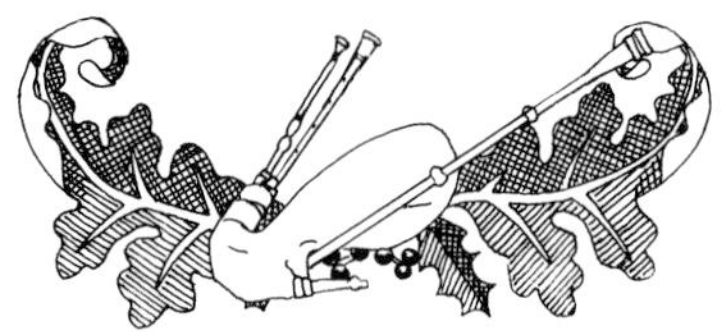

The skirl of the bagpipes could stir feet of clay.
The Scots march to war while the French dance and play,
But the drones and the chanters remind us this day
Of the flocks safe with shepherds in fields far away.

To amuse themselves at night, shepherds traditionally played pipes, which had developed from simple flutes by adding an animal skin or bladder as a reservoir for air. The player squeezes the bag to produce a continuous flow of air as he takes a breath for the blowpipe and fingers the flute, or chanter. The bagpipe could easily have been heard on the hills around Bethlehem on that first Christmas Eve. "Ut hoy!" sings the medieval carol about Jolly Wat, "the gude herdës boy. For in his pipe he made so much joy."

Suetonius, the Roman historian, wrote that Nero was adept with the instrument, and it has been suggested that it was a bagpipe that Nero played rather than a fiddle as Rome burned.

In the ninth century the bagpipe became part of the medieval revels, especially as an instrument for dance music. Medieval music was monophonic, having only a single line of melody, and the bagpipe suited it, most appropriately for round dances, called caroles.

By the thirteenth century, drones, which could produce only a single tone, were added to the bagpipe, resulting in the background hum that one associates with the instrument. As harmonic awareness developed and music grew polyphonic, the bagpipe declined. In Britain it became an instrument of the country folk. In Scotland, however, the fate of the bagpipe took a different turn. By the sixteenth century, due to the rousing effect it had on soldiers and the long distance that its sound carried, the bagpipe had become an instrument of war. (This quality caused the English to ban the bagpipe in Ireland, when dissident Irish began to protest the yoke of English rule.)

In France, as in other countries throughout Europe, the bagpipe continued to be popular as an accompaniment of dance. In the seventeenth century, a new bellows-driven (as opposed to mouth-blown) bagpipe was invented. Called the musette, it quickly became fashionable among French nobility. Musettes were sometimes elaborately crafted works of art, with ivory chanter, drones, and blowpipe and an outer bag cover often made of embroidered silk with fringe and tassels. The sound was said to be less shrill than the Scottish pipes. By the time of the French Revolution, hatred of the upper classes was so intense that the musette, with its aristocratic associations, disappeared forever. The cornemuse, however, a less refined bagpipe but one played by all levels of society, survived. The pipers shown in the painting are an itinerant band of French country musicians playing cornemuses in preparation for the Twelfth Night entertainment in this English country house.

Eleven ladies dancing

Stamp the earth! Awake! Awake!
Dance round the solstice fire.
Clockwise like the sun we turn
To banish winter's ire.

In midwinter in the late eighteenth century some English farmers still followed the old custom of lighting bonfires in their fields and celebrating noisily around them. These solstice fires had probably lost their association with the sun over the centuries, but the implied fertility rite still remained. After the fires went out, the rich ash was scattered over the fields to aid the spring growth. The dancers shown in the painting, always moving to the left, might have circled one of these fires, not knowing that the stamping of their feet came from an ancient rite for rousing the sleeping earth back to life.

Faced with a vast array of such pagan practices, the early Christian church, as it spread its teachings throughout the Roman Empire, condemned the old ways, unlike the Romans of old, who had tolerated and assimilated the religions of their conquered foes. Dance was considered one of the sins of the flesh and was believed to lead to sexual permissiveness, drunkenness, and lawlessness. To these early Christians, goodness was in the soul and dance was the devil's business.

One cleric observed that the common people danced to the left in a circle with the devil in the middle. In many cultures only right is considered good. In Latin, left is sinister; the English word is, of course, the same and means "suggesting an evil force." But the origins of leftward dancing are more easily explained: people danced to the left because round dances were performed in worship of the sun, whose journey from east to west was mimicked in the clockwise movement. In a like way the Egyptian astronomer-priests had circled the altar of their deity, the sun.

The sun similarly figures in many of the early rituals in which the center of the circle was a fire, a benevolent symbol of the sun's illumination, warmth, and purification. The dark side of sun worship was that fire was also an instrument of destruction, and some of the rituals associated with it used this dark side to entice the bright one to come forth. In some Celtic rituals the burnt offerings—gifts of appeasement for the gods—were very much alive during the ceremony. Since some of these offerings were human, the cleric's warning of there being a "devil in the middle of the circle" had an awful ring of truth.

Despite the assaults of Christianity, the round dance survived and, stripped of its heathen trappings, was tolerated throughout Europe. In France, the dance was called a carole, deriving from the Greek word chorus, which originally included not only singing but also ceremonial dance.

By the Middle Ages, the carole had found its way into court entertainments and was immensely popular at feasts, where the dancers occasionally asked the revelers to join them. The carole formed the dance steps of the choral refrain that accompanied the verses sung by the lead minstrel. After the Crusaders returned from the Holy Land with new visions of love and the sensuousness of life in the East, the courtly carole developed more sophisticated choreography and included songs about love and marriage as well as the virtues and exploits of honored guests.

In the fifteenth century, the word for the dance, carole, was replaced by "branle" and the carole came to be associated with songs, which later, with the addition of the Christmas story, were called Christmas carols. The round dance, although it fostered many other forms—including, in the sixteenth century, the jig—continued to be enjoyed, perhaps because of its simplicity.

Twelve lords a-leaping

Hey! Ho! For the Lord of Misrule!
Play us a tune or give us a fool.
Feasting and dancing, wassailing the crowd,
The company's merry, the revelry loud.

At the Roman festivals on which Twelfth Night celebrations were overlaid, a "king," chosen by chance, directed the merrymaking. Custom dictated that masters become servants and vice versa, soldiers be served by officers, and men dress variously as horned animals or women. Despite the fact that the church took a dim view of the proceedings, many customs carried over into the medieval period and became favored traditions at Christmas. At some point the mock king became the Lord of Misrule.

In medieval Britain, the lords a-leaping were undoubtedly participants in morris dances, an assortment of costumed ceremonial folk dances, often performed during the interludes between courses of the Christmas feasts. In one, a variation of the carole, the male dancers, their faces blackened, circled clockwise with stamping steps and jingling bells and, as the music of the pipes and tabors grew more vigorous, leapt high in the air. (Morris dances were probably named for the blackened faces of the dancers, though the dances predated the name. The word morris may be a corruption of Moorish.)

Rooted in rituals for fertility and for war, the leaping dances belonged to men. The purpose of these energetic exercises was to fan the flames of faith or rage for battle, so that the dancer reached a spiritual peak that elevated him above the inhibitions of normal behavior. (The word enthusiasm, derives from the Greek *entheosiasmos,* meaning "of having the god within one.") Rebirth was a concept common to both rites, reflecting the belief that as the earth died in winter and was miraculously reborn in spring, so man, too, might be reborn after death.

In Roman rites, the Salii, priests of Mars, the god of vegetation and war, leapt high in the air to induce the corn to grow. The height of the jump was supposed to imitate the proposed height of the corn. The costumes worn by the Salii included swords. One form of morris dancing also included swords. Twelve male dancers in two teams performed an intricate pattern, at the end of which the swords were "braided" together to form a Lock or Nut above the chief—a sort of ritual decapitation. The victim "dies" and is resurrected by the other dancers.

In other Morris dances, such as the Abbots Bromley Horn Dance, the performers wore antlers and sometimes animal skins like the Romans. Disguise in folk dance followed tradition, not personal fancy. It was a way of fooling the spirits that were believed to be abroad in a world where death and the devil were constant companions. The autumnal shedding of a stag's antlers and their regrowth in the spring was another ancient symbol of the cycle of the seasons.

By the eighteenth century, morris dancing had declined as an entertainment of the upper classes and had become a popular attraction at fairs and festivals. Many churches maintained their own teams.

The lords a-leaping at Twelfth Night celebrations probably danced the gavotte, a dance of French origin that could be accompanied by the drum and bagpipe and whose characteristic step was a "hop-step-step-jump." Its popularity lasted until the end of the eighteenth century.

It is interesting to note that the song, *The Twelve Days of Christmas,* was recorded for the first time by James O. Halliwell in 1842. He reported that it was performed by boys with blackened faces wearing animal skins.

The twelfth night cake

This prince of plum cakes for Twelfth Night,
Delicious artifice of white,
No longer hides good fortune's bean
For by this card, one's role is seen.

Cake, in ancient times, was concocted of the finest ingredients, representative of the year's bounty and reserved for special occasions. The Twelfth Night cake may be descended from the ianual, the biscuit reserved for Janus, the Roman two-faced god of the portal, who looked back to the past and forward to the future. The first sacrifice of the year was to Janus, for whom the month of January is named, and as the year turned, the Twelfth Night cake offered a hopeful portent of bounteous harvest and an ancient communion with the gods of the earth.

One Twelfth Night cake, described in a 1620 tract from Geneva, was an unusual mixture of flour, honey, ginger, and pepper, undoubtedly a tribute to the spice trade and a reflection of the social status of the host. Another recipe for the cake originated at the French court of Henry III in the sixteenth century. Similar to the kugelhopf, a light Alsatian pound cake, this was baked in an octagonal mold. The king's company was divided into groups of seven and the cake was cut into eight pieces, with a slice dedicated to God and given to the poor. These cakes were enormously popular at court and came to be called "gateaux des rois."

In England and on the Continent, Twelfth Night cakes traditionally contained a bean and sometimes a pea. When the cake was served, whichever man found the bean became "king," a sort of Lord of Misrule. The woman who found the pea was the "queen." With the "king's" toast the merrymaking could begin in earnest. (In England the election of the bean king is first mentioned in the reign of Edward II, who ruled from 1307 to 1327.)

Throughout Europe royal interest in Twelfth Night celebrations focused on the Christian holy day, Epiphany, on which it falls. In the western branch of the church the emphasis on Epiphany, which means manifestation, lay in the presentation of the Christ child to the Magi. By the third century, these New Testament "wise men from the East" had been transformed into kings by reinterpretation of Old Testament prophecies. By the sixth century, the kings were established personages in the Christmas story. The royal houses of Europe were only too delighted to associate themselves with Epiphany, and therefore Twelfth Night, and share in the reflected glory. The kings of France even went so far as to add the Magi to their family tree.

English cakes were different from those of Europe. The passion for dried fruit that began when it became readily available in the sixteenth century influenced the contents, resulting in a heavy, fruity mixture called a plum cake. By the eighteenth century, the plum cake had acquired a sugar icing, the outgrowth of a medieval "after the feast treat" for honored guests when sugar was a rare commodity. By 1558, when Elizabeth I ascended the throne, sugar was readily available. Along with sugar came a taste for almonds that dated from the Middle Ages, when they were variously employed in recipes and considered an aphrodisiac. Marchpane, a favorite confection of almonds also known as marzipan, was added to the top of the plum cake and covered with sugar icing, which preserved it. Adding gum tragacanth to the icing stiffened it so that it could then be shaped into elaborate decorations.

Not surprisingly, tearing apart such delightful and expensive masterpieces in the search of a bean and a pea became undesirable, and a substitute was found. At first, slips of paper were passed in a hat, and the "king and queen" were drawn by lot, along with other humorous personages who filled out a mock court. By the late eighteenth century, the slips of paper had become cards representing the Twelfth

Night characters. The king and queen were also represented as decorations for the top of the cake in the form of two removable crowns.

Taken altogether, the foods and entertainments of what was once a medieval feast formed a delightful sequence of events culminating in the final celebration of Twelfth Night—a fitting farewell to the old year and a welcome for the new.

It is all preserved in the seemingly childish verses of a game and song, *The Twelve Days of Christmas*. Although the origins lie couched in the traditions of the ancient world, the message—both pagan and Christian—is the same. As day follows night and spring follows winter, the belief in rebirth endures. It reaches back in time, far beyond the Christian traditions, back to a time when God was nature in the mind of man. There is a certain cosmic reassurance in the antiquity of this belief and in its tenacity—an everlasting hope that belongs to pagan and Christian traditions alike. As the New Year is welcomed in and the cycle of the seasons begins again, where there seemed to be an end, there is a new beginning. Surely that is one of the greatest promises of Christmas.